COME FORTH:

A Journey From the Shadows into View

A Poetry Collection

ANDREA M. RENFROE

xulon
PRESS

Dedication

Scribes who let fear paralyze and keep them from walking in their God given purpose as I did for years. I say to them as it was said to me, ***COME FORTH***!

Jeanne Schaufelberg

Your quiet boldness and sweet aura amazed me. There you were, a white woman, in the projects (Brick City) teaching African American youth about Jesus. The anointing upon your life empowered you to communicate the gospel in a way I was able to quickly grasp and understand. The magnitude of each message and the grace in your delivery compelled me to choose Christ above all at the tender age of eight. You made such an impression until Marquita and I asked if we could adopt you as another grandma, thus the name "Grandma Jeanne". The innocence and purity of it all brings me great joy and sweet peace.

People like you are so often forgotten and overlooked. You were not in a mega church pulpit, you weren't on television, and you weren't a household name in Christendom. You chose to forego many sought after attainments in this life such as marriage, children, career, and mainstream recognition to pursue Christ (Matthew 6:19-21). Nonetheless, you were and are wealthy above measure because your accolades and recognition come from heaven where it really counts (2 Corinthians 10:18).

I love, honor, and cherish you because I would not be the woman I am today had you not been a part of my life. I am a jewel in your heavenly crown and a part of your spiritual legacy. You will never be forgotten. Thank you Grandma Jeanne.

Table of Contents

Acknowledgments

Abba – Father God

Thank You for saving me not only from the enemy and the world, but for saving me from myself. Thank You for seeing fit that I experience *Come Forth* before I could release *Come Forth* and thank You for choosing me to be Your ready writer and mouthpiece. May my life glorify You, edify the body of Christ, and communicate the gospel to a lost and dying world. I am who I am only because You are *Ehyeh Asher Ehyeh*, "*I AM THAT I AM*"!

Telly, my handsome husband

I love and appreciate you for pushing me to complete this project. Thank you for having confidence in me when I couldn't muster up enough in and for myself. Thank you for being and staying by my side through the good and the bad, the ups and downs, the beautiful and the ugly. I am thankful to God that by His grace and mercy, we are not only still standing, but we are still standing together and standing strong! I look forward to His continued blessings upon us as we happily grow old together in Him! I love you, Mr. Renfroe!

A'Mia and Telly Jr

I never thought I'd be a mother, but God saw fit that I become one. You are my angels. Your smiles, hugs and laughter make my heart melt and your individual personalities keep me in awe of how versatile God is. I love you both beyond measure and pray that this finished work gives you hope to know that you can do <u>EVERYTHING</u> He has blessed you to accomplish if you would only keep Him first in all you do (Matthew 6:33) and believe Him for the manifestation of it (Mark 9:23).

Dana English

We were scheduled to meet at Starbucks. I ordered my favorite—a chocolate chip scone (warmed) and bottled water. I devoured my snack, looked over my notes, and thought about how the meeting would go. I was honored and thankful you agreed to meet with me. When you walked in, I was excited and nervous at the same time. Although I'd received confirmation it was time to get my first book underway, I was still a little uncertain about the publishing process itself. I was also uncertain about how helpful you would be. After all, I didn't know you personally, and I was a novice in the book-writing arena. Boy was I was pleasantly surprised. Many times, accomplished and successful people hoard useful information that can help others navigate the very waters through which they have already charted. Dana, you were the total opposite. You shared specifics about publishing, illustrations, the spoken word, and other pointers from your writing journey. Thank you for your assistance and support. Your example and encouragement moved me to launch out into a part of my destiny I did not previously have the know how to pursue.

Family and friends (biological and spiritual)

Thank you for your love, prayers, support, and encouragement. You've helped make this dream a reality. I love you!

Foreword

As Apostle and Pastors of Kingdom Outreach Ministries International (KOMI), in Okinawa, Japan, my wife Kimberly and I can attest and witness to the prophetic anointing and holy life style of Andrea Renfroe. While under our leadership, she served as Minister, Elder, Prophet, Administrator, Teacher, and Senior Elder in charge during times of our absence. She is a good and faithful daughter in the things of God. Over the years, we have prophetically spoken and witnessed prophecies spoken concerning the anointing upon her to pen documents as God gives her inspiration. It blesses us to see the manifestation of those prophetic words in this exceptional document, *Come Forth*.

Come Forth serves as a road map to righteous decisions and imparts sound moral principals while recommending good character development. Within its pages, you will find a compilation of poetic, humorous, and abstract yet inspirational writings that give forth nuggets of wisdom and guidance. Andrea chronicles the times and artfully presents real life experiences that include the good, the bad, and the down right ugly. Her writings can be seen as prophetic letters to Christianity, challenging it and its leaders to affect those they influence. It also challenges Christian leaders to correct their presentation of the church and its purpose, and to take hold of the truth, which is able to set them and others free. To those who are not Christian, the writings connect with everyday struggles and gives hope through Jesus, who is the Way, the Truth, and the Life.

As you read, you will also connect with the author hearing the personal experiences and testimonies of how she overcame life's circumstances and situations common to all of us. Our greatest joy in reading *Come Forth* was to see our daughter in ministry establish the Word of God as the foundation for her successes (and ways of success for others) in each of her writings.

This book is a great read. It is sure to promote and inspire life change, help you realize you can overcome the many challenges of life, and enable you to share the concepts with others who can benefit from them as well. It is our hope you will be moved to live "Zoe" life.

May God richly bless Andrea and her family. May He also cause her to prosper for her labor and obedience in writing this book to be a blessing to others.

> *"I charge thee therefore before God, and the Lord Jesus Christ, who shall judge the quick and the dead at His appearing and His kingdom; Preach the Word; be instant in season, out of season; reprove, rebuke, exhort with all long-suffering and doctrine. For the time will come when they will not endure sound doctrine;*

but after their own lust shall they heap to themselves teachers, having itching ears; and they shall turn away their ears from the truth, ..." (**2 Timothy 4:1-4**).

Proclaim the Word Elder

Apostle Joseph W. King and Pastor Kimberly A. King

Founders and Pastors, Kingdom Outreach Ministries International (KOMI)

Planted and provides oversight to:

KOMI, Okinawa, Japan

KOMI, Virginia (USA)

Judah Sunrise Ministries, Yaka, Okinawa, Japan

Zebulun Christian Outreach Center, Henoko, Okinawa, Japan

Introduction

"But He knows the way that I take [He has concern for it, appreciates, and pays attention to it]. When He has tried me, I shall <u>come forth</u> as refined gold [pure and luminous]."
Job 23:10 (AMP)

Although I've been writing for years, I never had a zealous desire to write books. I entertained the idea, but it was never a serious consideration. Truthfully, I did not have the faith to believe I could do it. I knew I could write. Yet, I didn't see writing as a gift or a call and I didn't think what I'd written was good enough to meet "publishing" standards or to attain what I thought was success. I settled with simply writing and sharing with very few people if any at all. Most times the reaction was the same, "when are you going to publish your work?" My response was always generic and void of faith, "I don't know" or "I will eventually". Even with the encouragement and confidence others had in me, I was still not convinced I could do it. But my outlook began to change in the fall of 2009. While attending a women's conference at my home church (Kingdom Outreach Ministries International), a prophetic declaration was released. At that moment, I received an impartation from the Lord and confirmation that it was time to write my first book.

Approximately one month later, I stood in the back of the sanctuary talking with my spiritual mother, Pastor Kimberly King. Amongst other things, she said; *"Daughter, it is time for your book to* **COME FORTH."** I was in agreement and "thought" I knew just how the book was going to come to fruition. By my account, I had enough material to write several books. I thought I'd gather **_EVERY_** poem and article I'd ever written, shove them into one manuscript, and be off to the races as a published author. Not only was I wrong, I was dead wrong. First off, all of my work was not meant to be restricted to one volume. Secondly, the fact there was a very real process between where I was and where I was going eluded me. I didn't realize before I could release a finished work according to God's mandate, I had to be worked on. Purification and refining were the order of the day and gobs of both were on my plate. Whew, what a hard pill (process) to swallow.

While establishing the manuscript for this book, I pondered what the essence of "come forth" really meant. Although the meaning was seemingly obvious, I did not want to be lopsided in my understanding. Furthermore, I did not want to overlook deeper meaning (if there was any). So I took the old fashion route and began to study. Of course I was unable to find a definition for the actual phrase "come forth". However, I was able to pinpoint a viable synonym; Emerge[1]:

- To come into view or notice, as from concealment or obscurity
- To come into existence; develop
- To rise, as from an inferior or unfortunate state or condition

The definitions were simple yet they spoke volumes to what was unfolding in my life and also served as glaring evidence of what the title of this book would be.

Throughout my life, Father has lovingly guided me along a path of discovery. He has shown me how I'd been hiding because of fear, doubt, and unbelief. He also revealed how He has purposefully hidden me for a kairos revealing and how He was using all things to shape and mold me (Romans 8:28 – my favorite scripture). However, the past five years have been very significant. God has divulged two very distinct aspects of my purpose: that of prophet and scribe, and how synergy between the two works to accomplish Kingdom purpose in the earth.

They say a journey begins with one step. I say a journey begins with a decision. My journey began in the mind of God. Before the foundations of the world, He decided I would be a scribal prophet. However, it

---

[1]   Emerge [Def. 1, 4, 5]. (n.d.). *Dictionary.Com Unabridged.* In Radom House. Retrieved January 9, 2014, from http://dictionary.reference.com/browse/emerging

wasn't until I embraced both components (even without a full intellectual understanding) that I was able to release this first finished work. I am grateful and better for my process thus far and I am looking forward with great expectation to what's ahead.

—Andrea M. Renfroe

"...And he said unto me, *Write*..." (Rev. 21:5, KJV).

My Brother's Keeper

"*I*'m my brother's keeper" is a phrase many tend to use loosely and when convenient. Unfortunately, it has become a mockery and a joke because actions, oftentimes, do not mirror words. The disparity causes unnecessary hurt and pain and pushes some away from the household of faith and worst, away from the Lord. Being our brother's keeper includes an array of examples. Yet, the common denominator is LOVE! Love is the standard that reveals whether we are our brother's keeper not just in word but also in deed.

A new commandment I give unto you, That ye love one another; as I have loved you, that ye also love one another. By this shall all men know that ye are my disciples, if ye have love one to another

(John 13:34-35, KJV).

...but by love serve one another (Galatians 5:13, KJV).

Bear ye one another's burdens, and so fulfil the law of Christ (Galatians 6:2 KJV).

With all lowliness and meekness, with longsuffering, forbearing one another in love...
(Ephesians 4:3, KJV).

Wherefore comfort yourselves together, and edify one another...
(I Thessalonians 5:11).

Holding up the Line

The commission has been given. Your orders are in affect.
The question of the day is: "Why haven't you acted yet?"

You know what to do. You know what to say.
But you haven't taken that step to get the mission underway.

Be My witnesses throughout the earth. Spread the good news in and out of season.
Minister to the hurt, the oppressed, and those stricken with diseases.

Boldly proclaim My word so the lost will be lost no more.
Shout it from the ends of the earth from coast to coast and shore to shore.

Walk in righteousness and do good; put on the mind of Christ.
Be upright in all of your ways. Communicate the gospel with your life.

With all diligence study the scriptures that you may be empowered and equipped.
Be filled and led by My Spirit, so you won't be exploited or tricked.

These instructions and so much more have I given. I'm waiting for you to act.

When you don't follow My orders, you hinder the progress of the ones in the back.

If you fail to encourage your sister, she ends up staying in her pit.
She, in turn, is incapable of helping others; her opportunity she has missed.

The ones she cannot help are hindered and remain in their condition.
Because the one up front held up the line, keeping them from being in their proper position.

We are all connected and we can directly or indirectly affect one another.
Don't allow what you do or lack thereof to hinder your sister or brother.

Pay attention and take heed. Are your ears inclined?
Be sure you are not the one holding up the line.

> *Let us not therefore judge one another any more: but judge this rather, that no man put a stumblingblock or an occasion to fall in [his] brother's way. [It is] good neither to eat flesh, nor to drink wine, nor [any thing] whereby thy brother stumbleth, or is offended, or is made weak (***Romans 14:13b & 21, KJV***).*

Meeting the Need

"Excuse me sir, can you give me directions? I'm trying to find my way. Started early this morning. Got my bags packed up, been traveling most of the day.

I figured I'd know which way to go when I got to this particular spot. But it seems I was wrong; I've erred on my journey. Thought I was on track. Truth is, I'm not."

"Sure I can help," said the passerby. "Just keep moving you'll eventually arrive."
The young man was confused. Those weren't directions at all, so he turned to another passerby.

"Excuse me ma'am, can you give me directions? I'm trying to find my way."
"Sure I can help," the woman said. "Here's a map, now you have a blessed day!"

The young man shook his head in disbelief. This was definitely not what he expected.
As he continued to ponder over his present dilemma, his thoughts were interrupted.

An old man walked up and said, "Young man, are you lost? Are you seeking help? Tell me what you need."

The young man replied, "I asked others for directions, but all I got was a map I can't read."

"Hand over the map and take a seat," said the old man. "I'll give you directions right to the front door.

I'll even show you the way. Just follow me. I've been on this very same journey before.

It took some time to make it through because sometimes people saw I was lost but they refused to help.

Other times people gave me information, but nothing with substance so I kept trying to find the way by myself.

I was worse off than when I first headed out. It seemed the more I tried the more lost I became.

Then one day a lady saw how lost I truly was and took honor in helping to relieve my pain.

She sat me down and gave me directions just like I'm doing with you today. She highlighted my path on a map I had received early on; then she got up and dutifully led the way.

Because she had traveled that same road before, she maneuvered it with mastery and ease.

Through her wisdom and understanding of my situation she was able to meet my need."

The older man looked upon the face of the younger and smiled as he slowly rose to his feet.

Then he turned on his heels and began to move forward. He was doing what it took to meet the need.

The next time someone is on a journey, in a situation, or dealing with a circumstance and you that way are passing,

don't just give directions, lead the way. Meet the need and be a blessing!

> *If a brother or sister be naked, and destitute of daily food, And one of you say unto them, Depart in peace, be ye warmed and filled; <u>notwithstanding ye give them not those things which are needful to the body; what doth it profit?</u> (James 2:15-16, KJV)*

Stay in your Lane

What do I do when I know something about a person's situation? Do I tell them or do I let it be?

Are there guidelines I should follow? Are there rules that apply when the circumstance has nothing to do with me?

Should I be a spectator, stand by and let them live? Do I shut my mouth and turn my head?

Don't they have a right to know what's going on, or will they be better off if nothing is said?

If I fail to inform them, if I don't share this information, will not destruction lay in the balance?

Will not heartbreak and suffering and pain beyond description be the end result of my silence?

Am I to speak up or should I digress? What is my responsibility and part to play in all of this?

When I'm around them, should I act as if nothing's wrong? Should everything I know simply be dismissed?

It's so confusing because I want to help; I don't want to see them endure unnecessary hardship.

But at the same time, I don't want to get involved and I'm not really sure how they'll handle it.

Wisdom is paramount. It's needed to discern. It can be the difference between a person's peace or their pain.
It's hard to know my place in someone else's affairs. Should or shouldn't I stay in my lane?

> *...get Wisdom (skillful and godly Wisdom)! [For skillful and godly Wisdom is the principal thing.] And with all you have gotten, get understanding (discernment, comprehension, and interpretation)* **(Proverbs 4:7, AMP).**

> *To every thing there is a season, and a time to every purpose under the heaven...a time to keep silence, and a time to speak...* **(Ecclesiastes 3:1 & 7, KJV).**

Crisis in the Body

There are numerous local churches in operation that, by their very acts, attempt to diminish the impact the global church and the Kingdom of God are making overall. Unfortunately, church is viewed as an elite society where membership places one in an elevated status. Leadership positions are sought after for selfish gain and prestige. Positive thinking and pseudo-empowerment messages replace anointed instruction that reveals God's character and breaks people out of spiritual prison cells. Leaders seek to be worshiped, while church members, through deception and erroneous teaching, move God off of the throne and replace Him with their idols, which are many times, their favorite pastor or leader. Agendas and programs restrict the Holy Spirit leaving people worse off than when they came to church. Conferences and other such services are on heavy rotation to distract from personal study of the Word and quality time with the Lord. Furthermore, religion and tradition are used to oppress the people and convince them that church attendance and church service trumps holiness and right relationship with Christ.

Despite this sad state of affairs, God is still in control. He has set a remnant in the earth that will tirelessly share His love and proclaim His unadulterated truth. They will not sit back and condone the mischiefs and foolishness that has subtly crept into the church through "people friendly, pleasurable, and modern" guises.

Are you ready to stand your ground for the cause of Christ and the real church or will you be seduced by the smoke screen called "church" behind which there is no real substance?

I decree and declare that order, peace, and divine alignment will swallow up crisis in the body.

> *Howbeit in vain do they worship me, teaching for doctrines the commandments of men. For laying aside the commandment of God, ye hold the tradition of men... Making the word of God of none effect through your tradition, which you have delivered; and many such things do ye* (**Mark 7:7-8 &13, KJV**).

> *...they exchanged the truth of God for a lie and worshipped and served the creature rather than the Creator... (Romans 1:25, AMP).*

...However, when they measure themselves with themselves and compare themselves with one another, they are without understanding and behave unwisely

(2 Corinthians 10:12, AMP).

For the time is coming when [people] will not tolerate (endure) sound and wholesome instruction, but, having ears itching [for something pleasing and gratifying], they will gather to themselves one teacher after another to a considerable number, chosen to satisfy their own liking and to foster the errors they hold."

(2 Timothy 4:3-4, AMP).

What's Wrong with this Picture?

~Past~

Two by two, that's how they were sent.

Two by two, they were instructed and went.

They turned the city out.

Change came without a doubt,

and the gospel continued to spread throughout the land.

~Present~

Hundreds of churches is the outfit.

A slew of pastors in the pulpit.

No spirit, no power, no change.

No freedom from binding chains.

Deliverance is far removed from both the saint and sinner man.

*And He called to Him the Twelve [apostles] and began
to send them out [as His ambassadors] two by two and
gave them authority and power over the unclean spirits.
And they went out, and preached that men should
repent. And they cast out many devils, and anointed
with oil many that were sick, and healed them*

(Mark 6:7, 12 & 13, AMP).

Now after this the Lord chose and appointed seventy others and sent them out ahead of Him, two by two, into every town and place where He Himself was about to come (visit) (Luke 10:1, AMP).

Having a form of godliness, but denying the power thereof... (2 Timothy 3:5, KJV).

Operation Clean House

I was sorely torn between one side and the other. I loved all and desperately wanted peace.

Various observations revealed what appeared to be strong was actually weak underneath.

Division, strife, favoritism, and partiality; subtle contamination poisoned individuals and thus the whole.

She's wrong, he's wrong, shifting the blame. Carnality in operation and flesh obviously in control.

Lord, what part do I play in this situation? What do I do and what would You have me say?

Approaching leadership is surely a fearful thing and addressing fellow members may push them away.

Some members have gone. Others stay but are confused and still others are ready to abandon ship.

I plead with You Lord to steady my feet. Make me steadfast and please don't let me slip.

Lord give me wisdom and grant unto me discernment. Reveal with clarity how to walk out my part.

Calibrate my spiritual eyes. Attune my spiritual ears. Expose, by Your Spirit, the intent of each heart.

I dare not downplay my involvement in any of this. If I've been wrong, cleanse my heart Lord and lay hot coals to my mouth.
Bring unity to the pieces as you sweep through this church body. Make manifest your glory as You clean this local house.

> *Now I beseech you, brethren, by the name of our Lord Jesus Christ, that ye all speak the same thing, and that there be no divisions among you; but that ye be perfectly joined together in the same mind and in the same judgment* (**1 Corinthians 1:10, KJV**).

Where are the Prophets?

Where are the prophets who will cry loud and spare not? Where is the voice of God throughout the land?
Have those who are called to be the mouthpiece of God afraid to confront and speak truth to mere man?

The prophets of old stood firm against wicked leaders. But many prophets today allow fear of man to be their driving force.
Meanwhile, corrupt leaders run rampant deceiving themselves and others taking God's glory and ignoring Him as their source.

The flock is led astray by the selfish ambitious of church leaders; God's will lost in the midst of carnal plans.
The weak and ignorant exploited. Their gifts, money and resources squandered to elevate and bring glory to man.

Where are the prophets who will cry loud and spare not? Where is the voice of God in the earth?
Have those who are called to be the mouthpiece of God afraid to shed light on leadership's dirt?

Where is John the Baptist; a voice crying in the wilderness, boldly proclaiming and preaching the message of repentance?

The one who fearlessly stood for truth as he confronted Herod with no looming worries about the majority's acceptance.

Where is Nathan, the one who without hesitation told David, "That guilty man happens to be you?"
Where is Samuel, the one who said to Saul, "You did not do everything God required of you?"

Where is Elijah, who stood in the strength of the Lord and challenged Ahab, Jezebel and the prophets of Baal?
Where are the prophets of today who will not be afraid to stand for truth so the word and will of God will prevail?

Where are the prophets who will cry loud and spare not concerning leadership's sins and iniquities?
Where are the prophets? Well I don't know about you but my response is: Lord, here I am send me!"

> *Also I heard the voice of the Lord, saying, Whom shall I send, and who will go for us? Then said I, Here am I; send me* (Isaiah 6:8, KJV).

> *Cry aloud, spare not, lift up thy voice like a trumpet, and shew my people their transgression, and the house of Jacob their sins* (Isaiah 58:1, KJV).

Check in the Box

Go to Sunday service ☑

Pray for an hour ☑

Listen to some word about Holy Ghost power ☑

Speak in tongues ☑

Sing praises and shout ☑

Receive instruction on casting devils out ☑

Memorize some verses ☑

Serve on a church board ☑

Implement the word to be effective for the Lord ☐

> *But be ye <u>doers</u> of the word, and not hearers only, deceiving your own selves (James 1:22, KJV).*

Shift

We can't stay in this familiar place any longer; surely it's time to move. Complacency and stagnation are looming overhead; there's a need for something new.

The ordinary is old and the common stale; progression has ceased to exist. Growth will continue to escape our grasp if we do not embrace this present shift.

> *Remember ye not the former things, neither consider the things of old. Behold, I will do a new thing...*
>
> > **(Isaiah 43:18-19, KJV).**

> *Brethren, I count not myself to have apprehended: but this one thing I do, forgetting those things which are behind, and reaching forth unto those things which are before, I press toward the mark for the prize of the high calling of God in Christ Jesus*
>
> > **(Philippians 3:13-14, KJV).**

Wake Up

Wake up from your sleep. Emerge from your slumber.
Arise from your snoozing. Snap out of your stupor.

The alarm has sounded. Did you hear the clarion call?
Snap to attention. Get up and on the ball.

Look out and see the darkness extending far and wide.
Perceive the world's condition with open, scale-less eyes.

Rampant evil on every hand; people desensitized.
No desire for the presence of God, astute in their own minds.

Wars internal and external. Conflicts at home and abroad.
Good labeled as evil an initiative noteworthy of Satan's applause.

Wake up from your sleep. Emerge from your slumber.
Arise from your snoozing. Snap out of your stupor.

The shofar sounds. The call is being released.
Do you hear and perceive or are you still asleep?

And that, knowing the time, that now it is high time to awake out of sleep: for now is our salvation nearer than when we believed (Romans 13:11, KJV).

Therefore let us not sleep, as do others; but let us watch and be sober. For they that sleep sleep in the night; and they that be drunken are drunken in the night. But let us, who are of the day, be sober, putting on the breastplate of faith and love; and for an helmet, the hope of salvation (I Thessalonians 5:6-8, KJV).

The Transformation Process

Change and transformation are necessary for growth, development and maturation. However, it should be understood that transformation is more than change; it is the culmination of various changes. In other words, transformation is the most distinct and pronounced manifestation of change. If you observe a tree in the summer, its leaves are green. In the fall, the leaves are bursting with vibrant golds, oranges, and browns. In the winter, the tree is leafless. Even though it is still a tree at each stage, it is clear that change occurred. Take the same tree, chop it down, and process it. It is now pencils, paper, a dresser, an entertainment center, or maybe even a china cabinet. Not only did the tree change, it was literally transformed. Its current state is such that it can never return to its former state. It has become more of itself.

So it is with our lives (natural and spiritual). We will have encounters and experiences that not only change us, they will transform us if we allow them to. Not only will we look different, we will be different. Our perspective, expression, behavior and thought processes will move beyond short term to long term, from temporal to eternal. In submitting to the transformation process, we progressively come forth into who God created us to be.

This section includes glimpses of my personal transformation process. I admittedly struggled with self-righteousness, unbelief, fear, unforgiveness, and the need for acceptance and validation. BUT GOD!!!!!! His love has transformed me from glory to glory that I would accept and express (with my life) who He is in me and who I am in Him.

> *And all of us, as with unveiled face, [because we] continued to behold [in the Word of God] as in a mirror the glory of the Lord, are constantly being transfigured into His very own image in ever increasing splendor and from one degree of glory to another; [for this comes] from the Lord [Who is] the Spirit*
>
> **(2 Corinthians 3:18, AMP)**.

Ain't Nobody Livin' Right Cept Me

~~~~~~Me~~~~~~

Ain't nobody livin' right 'cept me. Jesus himself would be proud.
I don't drink or smoke or fornicate. My Christlikeness speaks real loud.

Ain't nobody livin' right 'cept me. All my stuff is in line and intact.
My morals are high. My sins are low. Who has a record like that?

Ain't nobody livin' right 'cept me. I ain't after another woman's man.
I got my own. What I want with another? To be the wife of one husband
is the plan.

Ain't nobody livin' right 'cept me. Indulgence in pornography? No not I.
See no, hear no, and speak no evil. In my righteousness I take pride.

Ain't nobody livin' right 'cept me. I'm so tired of these people and their
foolishness.
Just outright sinful with no fear of God and no desire for righteousness.

~~~~~~God~~~~~~

Hold on!
Ain't nobody livin' right 'cept you? Is that the stance you choose?
Well if that's the case, because I'm judge, then the verdict is you lose.

If you want to get down to the true hard facts, ain't nobody livin' right—
not even you.
With your "I don't do this and I don't do that" self-righteous attitude.

All have sinned and fallen short of My glory. No one has passed the test.
So you are out of line and in contrast with My word when you brag about
your righteousness.

Every kind word you muster, every good deed you do, every time you
bypass wrong to do right,
It still falls short, it doesn't make the mark, and it's as filthy rags before
My sight.

There is a danger that surrounds self-righteousness. It's a cleverly dis-
guised sin.
It focuses on outward behavior and actions, yet it overlooks that which
is within.

No, you don't smoke or drink or fornicate. No, you don't indulge in
pornography.
But you do hold grudges; your thought process is tainted, among other
hidden impurities.

You stand in judgment of your brothers and sisters while at the same time
refusing to forgive.

Living right also includes the condition of the heart it's not exclusively about how you live.

So the next time you want to take on the spirit of a Pharisee and declare, "Ain't nobody livin right 'cept me!"
Be quick to confess your sins, repent on the spot, and take a sober self-inventory.

> *But we are all as an unclean thing, and all our righteousnesses are as filthy rags* **Isaiah 64:6, KJV**).

> *For I say, through the grace given unto me, to every man that is among you, not to think [of himself] more highly than he ought to think; but to think soberly, according as God hath dealt to every man the measure of faith* (**Romans 12:3, KJV**).

Whose Sin is Greater?

Look at her with those tight shorts on; flesh bustin' loose in all directions.
Flirting non-stop, the men are lusting so she proceeds with no discretion.

Those lusting men, their minds on go. The fantasies start to form.
They fail to take time to cast down those thoughts, instead going with the fleshly norm.

He laughs and smiles at his darling wife with love. She is his joy and his delight.
How quickly he changes into an adulterer when he leaves her line of sight.

She cooks and cleans and loves her kids. Her heart belongs to her husband only.
But when he's away, she has eyes for another because she is feeling lonely.

He's at church every Sunday, his spirit so gentle. He loves to serve the Lord above.
But when he goes home, it's not to a wife. Instead, it's a man who gets his love.

She regularly ministers and feeds the hungry. She sings, mentors and assists.

But in the darkness of the night, in the basement of her house, at her hands the abuse of her children persists.

He has no remorse for the rape and murder he committed. He could care less that she left a family behind.
All he knows is that he's glad she's dead and in his mind, he is justified.

Her actions are pure. She's as righteous as they come. No blame can be pinned upon her.
But no one can see the condition of her heart, which is contaminated with resentment and anger.

They shout in every service. "Preach, preacher", they say. My God, they can pray and plead the blood.
But they live like devils all week long and they refuse to show forth love.

Whose sin is greater? Who is most guilty? Who has done the unthinkable thing?
Is it his sin or her sin or my sin or your sin? Whose slate is actually clean?

To God, sin is sin no matter what the deed and no matter what the size:
adultery, fornication, homosexuality, murder, slander and getting high;
abuse, unforgiveness, harboring anger, bad attitude, cursing and lust;
lying, stealing, gossiping, back-biting and betraying another's trust.

All sin is equal in the sight of the Lord. No one sin is greater than the next. God's outlook on the matter is very simple, yet we make it so complex.

We think a little wrong is in no way detrimental. "No big deal," so we say. A little, a lot, a lot, a little, by God's standard it's all wrong either way.

When you think you're better then someone else because you didn't do what they did,

remember that no matter how minute or irrelevant it may seem, to God, sin is still sin.

So I ask again:

Whose sin is greater? Who is most guilty? Who has done the unthinkable thing?

Is it his sin or her sin or my sin or your sin? Whose slate is actually clean?

> *Now the works of the flesh are manifest, which are these; Adultery, fornication, uncleanness, lasciviousness, Idolatry, witchcraft, hatred, variance, emulations, wrath, strife, seditions, heresies, Envyings, murders, drunkenness, revellings, and such like: of the which I tell you before, as I have also told you in time past, that they which do such things shall not inherit the kingdom of God* (Galatians 5:19-21, KJV).

Searching for Peace

I am searching through the clutter within the confines of my brain.
My sanity, right now, is getting harder to maintain.

I keep moving forward as the pressure continues to mount.
Minutes turn into days. I am slowly losing count.

I struggle to find peace, as chaos and calamity rise.
When I think everything is okay then up jumps the surprise.

I'm having problems with my health, in my family and at work, too.
My breaking point is near. Oh, what to do? Oh, what to do?

From somewhere deep inside, I hear a still small voice say:
"Stop! Go no further. Get on your knees and pray.

Your power is incapable of keeping you through your tests.
You can only do so much. Let Me handle the rest.

You've been physically trying to push your way through these present trials.
The flesh can only take you so far, but My Spirit will take you unlimited miles.

Stop trying to do My job. I've been in control since the beginning of time.

Why would I allow disaster and defeat to consume that, which is mine?

I made a promise to give you rest. I made a promise to give you peace.

I declared that it was you whom I'd never forsake or leave.

Now, take Me at My word! Allow Me to rule and reign.

If your mind is stayed on Me, peace you will obtain."

> ***Thou wilt keep him in perfect peace, whose mind is stayed on thee: because he trusteth in thee*** **(Isaiah 26:3, KJV).**

People Pleasing

Their words use to send me plummeting into an abyss of self-hatred. Their actions use to activate a low self-esteem curse.

I'd second-guess myself because of their lofty stares and demeaning attitudes. I was ignorant of my worth.

The need for their approval use to keep me up at night pondering ways in which I could satisfy and please.

The yearning for acceptance kept my soul ensnared. Running myself ragged to ensure everyone around me was appeased.

Fear of rejection contaminated my thoughts. It crushed me from without and consumed me from within.

It kept me bowed down to the wants and need of others. I couldn't please God. I was too busy pleasing them.

Much of my time was wasted worrying about the opinions of others and conforming to what they wanted me to be.

Along the way I lost sight of who and what was most important: my heavenly Father and His thoughts toward me.

> *Now am I trying to win the favor of men, or of God? Do*
> *I seek to please men? If I were still seeking popularity*

with men, I should not be a bond servant of Christ (the Messiah) (Galatians 1:10, AMP).

Whatever may be your task, work at it heartily (from the soul), as [something done] for the Lord and not for men, knowing [with all certainty] that it is from the Lord [and not from men] that you will receive the inheritance which is your [real] reward. [The One Whom] you are actually serving [is] the Lord Christ (the Messiah) (Colossians 3:23-24, AMP).

For I know the thoughts and plans that I have for you... (Jeremiah 29:11a, AMP).

How precious also are thy thoughts unto me, O God! how great is the sum of them! (Psalm 139:17, KJV)

My Worst Enemy

At first she was cool. No worries with her. She didn't raise any suspicion.

She was nice and friendly; she smiled when she saw me.

She was far removed from confusion and contention.

She reassured me. She was definitely there for me. I looked to her to calm my nerves.

She gave without expectation. She showed love. No condemnation.

To me, she offered compassion and an encouraging word.

A constant barrage of hurtful words and actions came from some closest to me.

She could no longer withstand the pressure. She tried to fight for me, but it weakened her.

She changed and became a monster eventually.

Instead of being there for me as she once was, she began to judge and criticize.

No longer did she exhort me. She was now hurting me.

I became nothing and unworthy. I was the enemy in her eyes.

She would never let me rest. She was constantly on my back.

Making me feel bad, bringing up hurts from my past.

I didn't know whether to retreat in fear or to boldly react.

She was a ravenous animal. She tried to consume me. She wanted me to die.

She worked hard for my demise. She attacked my body, my soul and my mind.

I couldn't figure out what was going on. So I had to ask her "WHY?"

She gave an explanation that was shocking to say the least. It shook me to the core.

She was honest, blunt and crude. She was vulgar, mean and rude.

She had become what she was because of the pain and suffering she saw me endure.

Watching me hurt and not being able to make it better took a toll on her.

She said she tried, but she failed. She cried, she hollered, she wailed.

She was hardened because of her lost attempts to make sure I didn't suffer.

My hurt and pain totally skewed her outlook and distorted her original make-up.

Her love became hate. Her patience became "don't wait."

She wanted every offender to pay. Doing good was an option she wanted to give up.

When I thought about what she said and looked at what had taken place, it totally blew me away.

The truth was now here. Everything became clear.

"She" was really me. I was my own worst enemy!

Looking diligently lest any man fail of the grace of God; lest any root of bitterness springing up trouble you, and thereby many be defiled... (Hebrews 12:15, KJV).

"As I walked out the door toward the gate that would lead to my freedom, I knew if I didn't leave my bitterness and hatred behind, I'd still be in prison."

~Nelson Mandela

"I know from personal experience how damaging it can be to live with bitterness and unforgiveness. I like to say it's like taking poison and hoping your enemy will die."

~ Joyce Meyer

"I count him braver who overcomes his desires than him who conquers his enemies; for the hardest victory is over self."

~ Aristotle

Tried and Proved

I thought I was on a roll. I just knew everyone I could save.

As long as I fervently, from the heart shared the word and illuminated the way.

Every question I answered with "JESUS" because nothing and no one else would do.

No problem was unsolvable as long as I presented Jesus to you.

I was quick to jump into a conversation if Jesus was being discussed.

My Lord and Savior fully satisfied me. He was much more than enough.

If a brother or sister in Christ was in close proximity to me,

In the midst there'd be spontaneous celebration: a Holy Ghost party!

It was no problem to lay hands on my children and pray fevers away.

I thought Satan was running scared because he knew I DIDN'T PLAY!

But little did I know that around me was a shield of angels forming a spiritual wall.

God had purposefully positioned this hedge of protection so that I wouldn't slip or fall.

He had been keeping me safe from danger and keeping the er

My time of testing hadn't yet come. However, it wasn't too far away.

Then one day it happened. The hedge round about me was lifted and removed.

It was my time to be tested. It was my time to be tried and proved!

I cried out, "Why Father is this happening to me? Why is everything falling apart?"

He replied, "My child, I am building your character. I am strengthening your heart.

I am allowing these things to happen so you can grow, develop and mature.

This way you can minister not on what someone told you, but on what you know is sure.

How can you tell someone I am able if I didn't do it for you?

How can you tell someone they can make it if I never brought you through?

You have to go through the problem before you can say the solution works.

Prior to the victories, you must experience the accompanying pain and hurt.

Growth and maturity are vital and very necessary. Being proven is the costly price.

For how can you effectively communicate the gospel if you do not grow in Christ?

Rest in knowing that your tribulations are ultimately for My glory and for the greater good.

Go through and endure the situation, even when it is not easily understood.

I am bringing you to a place that you cannot even imagine and your mind can't comprehend.

But I have to form and shape your character and it's going to start from within.

I will burn and strip away some things and add some things in their place.

I will prune and purge you continually until I no longer see you, but Jesus's face.

Take heed My child and listen closely because this is meant for you.

Your test will be your testimony if, through Me, you are tried and proved!"

Beloved, think it not strange concerning the fiery trial which is to try you, as though some strange thing happened unto you: But rejoice, inasmuch as ye are partakers of Christ's sufferings; that, when his glory shall be revealed, ye may be glad also with exceeding joy

(I Peter 4:12-13, KJV).

I Am Who I Am

I am who I am because of where I've been and where I am destined to go. I am who I am because of what I've learned and what I am destined to know.

I am who I am because of what I've experienced. I am who I am because of what I've suffered.
My physical, emotional and spiritual muscles have been strengthened. Life's obstacles have made me tougher.

I am who I am because of rejection. I am who I am because of betrayal and ridicule.
My faith has been stretched. Patience is doing a perfect work. I've learned to use my pain as a tool.

I am who I am because of what I've heard. I am who I am because of what I've seen.
I've been through hell and during the journey character is what I've gleaned.

Moreover [let us also be full of joy now!] let us exult and triumph in our troubles and rejoice in our sufferings, knowing that pressure and affliction and hardship produce patient and unswerving endurance. And endurance (fortitude) develops maturity of character (approved faith and tried integrity). And character [of this sort] produces [the habit of] joyful and confident hope of eternal salvation (Romans 5:3-4, AMP).

I Have and Still...

I have lived and still I'm living.

I have learned and still I'm learning.

I have grown and still I'm growing.

I have become and still I'm becoming.

I Have and Still...

Being confident of this very thing, that he which hath begun a good work in you will perform it until the day of Jesus Christ (Philippians 1:6, KJV).

Decisions, Decisions, Decisions

Leave or stay?

Pursue or abandon course?

Trail blaze or give way?

Shrink back or come forth?

I am able to do nothing from Myself [independently, of My own accord—but only as I am taught by God and as I get His orders]. Even as I hear, I judge [I decide as I am bidden to decide. As the voice comes to Me, so I give a decision], and My judgment is right (just, righteous), because I do not seek or consult My own will [I have no desire to do what is pleasing to Myself, My own aim, My own purpose] but only the will and pleasure of the Father Who sent Me (John 5:20, AMP).

Come Forth

From the shadows into view, from the darkness into light
I am emerging from obscurity into a future assured and bright.

Ascending from oppression. Shaking loose from insignificance.
Walking in my call knowing I was destined to make a difference.

No longer on the backside. No longer covered up and tucked away.
Unveiled and released for this generation, for this time, and for this day.

I will stand on my rampart and wait for what God will entrust to me.
Then I will boldly decree with my voice and pen what I hear and what I see.

> *Before I formed thee in the belly I knew thee; and before*
> *thou camest forth out of the womb I sanctified thee, and*
> *I ordained thee a <u>prophet</u> unto the nations*
> **(Jeremiah 1:5, KJV).**

> *Then said he unto them, Therefore every <u>scribe</u> which*
> *is instructed unto the kingdom of heaven is like unto a*
> *man that is an householder, which bringeth forth out of*
> *his treasure things new and old* **(Matthew 13:52, KJV).**

But He knows the way that I take [He has concern for it, appreciates, and pays attention to it]. When He has tried me, I shall <u>come forth</u> as refined gold [pure and luminous] (**Job 23:10, AMP**).

Special Thanks

Prophetess Vanessa Currie' Warren

In 2006, I was in the troughs of adversity and encountering the refiner's fire. While being pruned and purged, God divinely connected me to Prophetess Warren. Her impartation was unique in that it didn't come as a result of long and frequent periods of instruction. However, when I had the opportunity to be in her company, there was always (and still is) an expedient and substantial download. Under her watch, I entered into an intense season of training in the areas of intercession and spiritual warfare. During this season, the word of the Lord came on several occasions to reveal the prophetic aspect of my purpose. But I struggled with receiving the word each time feeling as if I could not operate at such a capacity in God. Nonetheless, Prophetess Warren continued to (and still does) thoroughly teach me and nudge me towards destiny. Her diligence, obedience and example have truly blessed me, enhanced my life, and caused me to stabilize in the call.

Apostle Joseph and Pastor Kimberly King

In 2009, Pastor Kimberly King recognized the prophetic anointing on my life and that it had been lying dormant. She quickly placed a demand on the anointing and called me out and called me forth. Some months later, I began leadership training under the tutelage of Apostle and Pastor King. Over time, they entrusted me with increasing responsibility in the ministry and placed more demands on the prophetic anointing for the cause of proper training and development. What blesses me most about my spiritual parents is their genuine love for people, their desire to connect people to Jesus first and subsequently to purpose, and their willingness to provide opportunities for those under their care to grow and mature in their gifts and calls. I love and appreciate them both for being an example of what true Godly leadership looks like.

Apostle Theresa Harvard-Johnson

In 2010, I came across an article written by Apostle Theresa Harvard-Johnson. I was immediately drawn by the distinctness of the writing and the authority it carried with it. It was as if God allowed Apostle Johnson to write the article just for my eyes and ears (RHEMA). Thereafter, I sought out more of her material and found she had a ministry specific to scribes, Voices of Christ Literary Ministries International where she passionately teaches that scribes are much more than just writers.

Although I'd never met her in person, little by little, God used Apostle Johnson to instruct me (by way of her literary works) in scribal ministry. Answers manifested for long standing questions I'd been asking myself. "Why do I love words, what they mean, and how they are used? Why is the way a pen or pencil writes such a big deal to me? Why am I so inclined to journal and write everything down (details, time, and date)? Why does it bother me if information is not presented in an orderly fashion? Why does injustice move me to action mainly to write and speak against the injustice and rouse the appropriate people to action? Why do I loathe erroneous teaching of the Scriptures? Why am I drawn to all things administrative?" As the "WHY's" married with their corresponding answers, I found peace, hope, understanding, and most importantly, I connected with purpose yet again.

Fast forward to October 2013. My hunger and thirst for revelation concerning scribal ministry was expansive. I desperately desired to attend something, anything hosted by Apostle Johnson and Voices of Christ Literary Ministries International to learn more. Previous attempts to attend a gathering were unsuccessful. Nonetheless, when God deemed I was ready and kairos knocked, I rushed to the door. I attended the 2013 Prophetic Scribal Advance in McDonough, Georgia. During this destined, intimate, and awesome time of exchange, Father God exceeded my expectations. He thrust me over the proverbial edge into a calibrated mind and renewed passion. Needless to say, I left Georgia ready to finish several scribal assignments I allowed to linger as a result of fear and complacency. The primary assignment being to complete and publish *Come*

Forth which would serve as the first published work of my scribal ministry - The Prophetic Pen.

Along life's journey, God connects us with people who not only challenge us to know what we are called to do but they also challenge us to actually walk it out. Prophetess Warren, Apostle King, Pastor King, and Apostle Harvard-Johnson are part of a divinely structured team of people God has used and is still using to do this very thing in my life.

THANK YOU!

The LORD bless thee, and keep thee: The LORD make his face shine upon thee, and be gracious unto thee **(Numbers 5:24-25, KJV).**

About the Author

Andrea M. Renfroe is a scribal prophet by the unmerited favor of God. He has given her the ability to skillfully paint word pictures with her pen (a weapon of warfare) to express His heart, encourage the oppressed, bring liberty to the bound; and present paradigm shifts where old patterns have caused stagnation. Andrea is committed to completing the work Father God has anointed and sent her to do (John 4:34). In that effort, she has set her face like flint to level every lie of the enemy released in her sphere of influence that blinds people to the love of Jesus Christ, belittles who Christ is in them, and contends with the understanding of their Kingdom purpose.

Look for these upcoming projects from Andrea

Inspired: A Narrative and Poetry Collection
Let Us Pray: Devotional and Prayer Journal
All Things Work Together: A Novel

⁘

To order additional copies of this book or for more information,
please email us or check out our website:

E-mail: thepropheticpen@yahoo.com
Website: www.thepropheticpen.com

CPSIA information can be obtained at www.ICGtesting.com
Printed in the USA
BVOW07s2125220614

356962BV00001B/2/P